THE AMERICAN NEWSPAPER

THE AMERICA TODAY SERIES

the
american
newspaper

ALVIN SILVERMAN

ROBERT B. LUCE, INC. WASHINGTON, D.C.

AMERICA TODAY Series No. 5

THE AMERICAN NEWSPAPER

Library of Congress Catalog Card Number: 64-19602

Manufactured in the United States of America

WESTERN PRINTING AND LITHOGRAPHING COMPANY
Cambridge, Maryland

Cover Design by STEPHEN KRAFT

Photographs courtesy of The Cleveland *Plain Dealer,* The Washington *Star,* and the Washington *Daily News.*

TABLE OF CONTENTS

THE AMERICAN NEWSPAPER

INTRODUCTION

At least once a year, the Kansas City *Star's* Roy A. Roberts, a distinguished editor, publisher, and reporter, returns to Washington, D.C. He comes partly to write of the people and places he knows so well. But the primary purpose of his visit is, in his own words, "to get the old battery of patriotism recharged."

Roberts began covering the Washington scene more than half a century ago. When he first came, he strode the Pennsylvania Avenue pavements in what was then an easygoing, sleepy town. There were only four other newsmen assigned to the White House, and on many days they had nothing to report. Today, there are more than 1,200 correspondents possessing White House credentials. Although many of them also cover the Congress, the Supreme Court, and other government departments, several hundred devote themselves completely to reporting only the activities of the President. Today's "saturation coverage" of the White House—compared with the presence of only five reporters fifty years ago—provides some indication of the vast changes in both the role of the federal government and in the development of the American newspaper.

In 1914, only the large press services and one or two New York newspapers bothered regularly to cover foreign policy news at the Department of State, then sharing the same picturesque Victorian structure with the War and

Navy Departments. Today, there are more correspondents from Great Britain alone covering the State Department than there were reporters in Washington when Ray Roberts first arrived. In 1964, a visitor could easily get lost in the endless corridors of the magnificent new building that houses the Department of State—a building that is already too crowded to accommodate all those who make and execute United States foreign policy.

This big government, representing the people of the United States, has poured out a greater flood of ideas and information than any government in the world at any time in history. As the major spokesman for the free world, the United States has always attempted to champion liberty without forcing its will on others. Helping to insure that this goal is understood by everyone is a remarkable institution that is at once a participant and observer, a supporter and critic of government: the American newspaper.

Roy Roberts is not the only prominent newspaper publisher who regularly comes to the nation's capital to stay in touch with the national mood and to make sure that his Washington bureau is providing readers with a fair and intelligent diet of news. The writer's own publisher-editor, Thomas A. Vail of the Cleveland *Plain Dealer,* makes frequent trips to Washington in order to fulfill his responsibility to the newspaper's readers. He, and other conscientious publishers like himself, attend background briefings at the State and Defense Departments and at the White House, meet with Senators and Congressmen, get to know Cabinet officials and representatives of other countries.

As a result, their newspapers can better fill their roles as accurate reporters of the government's day-to-day activities—as free and independent journals of our time. It is this independence upon which the American press prides itself. Our newspapers are responsible to no one except the people who read them. No paper in the United States speaks officially for the government or is told what or what not to publish in its columns. All are free to criticize anything about government, or anyone in government—from the President down.

In order to discover how this tradition of a free press grew up in the United States, let us travel back in history and trace the development of the American newspaper.

I

273 YEARS OF HISTORY

Newspapers and journalism had a slow start in America. During the Colonial period, the local governors representing the British crown placed strict limitations on publishing. Even the printing of Bibles, psalm books, and primers required licenses that were difficult to obtain. Further, the colonists had more urgent and immediate problems: defending themselves against warlike Indians, clearing forests, and planting crops. Even if news journals had been available, few people would have had the leisure to read them. Finally, printing equipment was scarce and expensive in the New World. Under these conditions, there was neither real need nor a real chance for a newspaper.

Colonial Period: 1690–1765. On September 25, 1690, seventy years after the first colonists arrived in America, Benjamin Harris, the proprietor of a Boston bookstore and coffeehouse, broke the literary silence in America with the first issue of his unlicensed four-page *Publick Occurrences Both Forreign and Domestick*. It was filled with news and provocative opinions. On the one hand, Harris charged Louis XIV, the French king, with immorality. On the other, he assailed the Mohawk Indians, allies of the British, for their savage treatment of French prisoners. This last accusation so enraged the governor of colonial Massachusetts that he issued a proclamation suppressing the paper and strictly outlawing any other unlicensed publications.

The first issue of *Publick Occurrences* was the last. But Harris's paper was the forerunner of a great line of American newspapers—publications that have made this country the most news-conscious society in the world.

For twenty-four years, no other paper appeared in the colonies. Finally, on April 24, 1714, the Boston postmaster, John Campbell, secured a license and printed the relatively mild Boston *News-Letter.* It was to continue for the next seventy-two years.

Five years later, two other papers appeared almost simultaneously. The Boston *Gazette* was first circulated on December 21, 1719, and somehow managed to survive despite the fact that it served as a platform for the views of such prominent Boston patriots as John and Samuel Adams and John Hancock. (Later, during the American Revolution, it was to become an outstanding and vigorous anti-British journal.) The next day, December 22, 1719, Andrew Bradford of Philadelphia founded the first American paper to be published outside of Boston, the *American Weekly Mercury.*

On August 7, 1721, still another Boston paper was born, and with it came a great improvement in the quality of Colonial journalism. Benjamin Franklin's half brother James founded the *New England Courant,* which followed the lively style of the Addison and Steele papers in England. The *Courant,* to which Benjamin Franklin was a major contributor, was the first American newspaper directly to criticize royal power and to encourage controversial letters from its readers. It was also more literary in tone than its predecessors and contemporaries, including essays, verse, and articles on manners and the arts that entertained as well as informed its readers.

William Bradford, the sixty-five-year-old father of Andrew Bradford (who had founded the *American Weekly Mercury*), thought he could do as well as his son and established the New York *Gazette,* which became an organ of the Royalist elements in America, and the first newspaper to be published in New York. Naturally this left the door open for an opposition paper. A German immigrant, John Peter Zenger, leaped at the opportunity with his New York *Weekly Journal.* Zenger charged that the Colonial government was corrupt in its practices and arbitrary in its methods. In 1734 Zenger was imprisoned for publishing seditious libel. A sensational trial followed, one of the most stirring events in the history of American journalism. The celebrated lawyer, Alexander Hamilton, went to New York from Philadelphia to defend Zenger. He did not deny that Zenger had written offending material, but argued that what Zenger had said was true. The judge was outraged and refused to admit such a defense. Hamilton turned to the jury and said, "Gentlemen, it is to you we must now appeal." The jury found Zenger not guilty, and he was set free.

Zenger's contribution was a significant one: he brought strong editorial opinion into its proper role in American journalism and thus opened the door to the next phase of American newspaper development.

Revolutionary Period: 1765–1783. Through the Stamp Act of 1765, the British crown required the use of expensive revenue stamps on all Colonial newspapers, almanacs, commercial and legal documents, and pamphlets. In the beginning, only lawyers and publishers objected to it. The issue loomed larger, however, when the colonists were made to realize that, for the first time, the British crown had found a means of taxing them directly. Raising the cry "taxation without representation," the colonials sent delegates to a Stamp Act Congress to decide what to do about this situation. The Congress voted to boycott English goods. Before long, British merchants and manufacturers felt the economic effects of the boycott and in March, 1766, finally persuaded Parliament to repeal the Stamp Act.

But it was too late. The Stamp Act, coupled with the Quartering Act, the Townshend Acts, and the Intolerable Acts, built up anti-British feeling in America to a fever pitch.

As early as 1772, the Boston *Gazette* and the *Massachusetts Spy* were openly discussing the possibility of a war for independence. This started a heated editorial debate in each of the colonies where every large city had its pro-British and anti-British journals. The anti-British editors were not only themselves outspoken, but offered their column space to patriotic writers. Thomas Paine, for example, used the *Pennsylvania Journal* for his celebrated "Crisis" papers. Ideas about independence already fermenting in the minds of many citizens at last appeared in print and were widely circulated.

The Revolutionary War, in which the colonists fought for their freedom from Britain, began on April 19, 1775, and ended officially eight years later. The thirteen British colonies became an independent nation, the United States of America.

Partisan Period: 1783–1830. The post-revolutionary period became known as the "Age of Party Papers"—and properly so. Not long after the signing of the Constitution in 1789, the founders of the infant republic became embroiled in a debate over whether or not to ratify (approve) the document. The Federalists, headed by Alexander Hamilton, supported approval but argued that the Constitution called for a central government that was not strong enough. Jefferson's anti-Federalists, or Republicans, argued against ratification by asserting that the federal government as organized in the Constitution was *too* strong, wielding a power that would mean the ultimate destruction of individual liberties.

Each party had a paper of its own. John Fenno, a Boston schoolteacher, was named editor of the Federalist *Gazette of the United States* in 1789, one year after Hamilton, James Madison, and John Jay had published their *Federalist Papers* in New York's *Independent Journal.* Jefferson, on his side, launched Philip Freneau, "the poet of the Revolution," into the editorship of the *National Gazette* in 1791. Even after the Constitution had been ratified, arguments continued about strong central government versus states' rights, and about the extent to which the federal government should exercise its powers. The dispute is still with us.

Throughout those early days, the Federalist-Republican controversies kept journalistic tempers boiling; newspapers sided with either Jefferson or Hamilton. Even George Washington smarted under insinuations and vilification from the opposition press. Fortunately, this violent and abusive journalism did not succeed. Publishers had learned that dignity and impartiality, at least in the presentation of news, were the most enduring qualities of a solid press.

After this, the American daily paper, as we know it today, began to take shape.

The economy of the young nation was beginning to thrive. Merchants needed the latest reports about trade, shipping, and agriculture. They also needed a medium in which to advertise their products to the public. The stage was set for a paper that would appear every day and provide these services for its readers. The *Pennsylvania Evening Post and Daily Advertiser,* the *Pennsylvania Packet and Daily Advertiser,* and the New York *Daily Advertiser* were three of the most prominent daily papers They carried some political news, but politics was decidedly subordinate to the economic events of the day. They were printed on large blanket-sheets and usually sold for six cents a copy. Until 1833, these dailies set the standard for American papers.

Penny Press Period: 1830–1860. The social and literary climate of America changed radically after 1830, and as the country changed, so did the newspapers. Free education extended literacy and with it came a hearty appetite for the news. Succeeding waves of immigration brought poorer laboring classes, mostly Irish and German, to this country, and the beginnings of industrialization brought more power and speed to printing machines.

New Year's Day, 1833, was a turning point in American journalistic history, for it saw the birth of the modern newspaper: Horace Greeley's New York *Morning Post,* the first "penny paper" in the United States. Actually, because of a fierce snowstorm the *Morning Post* did not survive the day, but an imitator, the New York *Sun,* founded a few days later by Benjamin H. Day, rocketed the penny paper into national popularity. It was written in a lively style and broke with journalistic custom by covering such colorful topics as police activities, court cases, "human interest" stories, crimes, and fires.

Two years after the *Sun* was founded, an ill-mannered, conceited, and eccentric man named James Gordon Bennett burst into the American newspaper scene to establish the New York *Morning Herald.* With five hundred dollars in his pocket and a makeshift desk in a cellar, Bennett prepared and printed a four-page penny paper with coverage as broad as the range of human affairs. In six weeks the circulation of the *Morning Herald* shot up to 7,000 daily. Bennett and his staff covered theatres, society, race tracks, and other sporting events. He maintained representatives in Washington and in the European capitals, and even purchased a fleet of small boats to meet incoming vessels in order to get stories faster. He was one of the first publishers to recognize the value of the telegraph to transmit news rapidly. Foreign correspondence, financial articles, full texts of important speeches, and lively accounts of everyday events were almost unknown before the *Herald*. These features were so popular that other editors immediately adopted them. After Bennett's death, his son, James Gordon, Jr., invented his own ways of "making news" for the *Herald*. At his own expense, he sent Henry Morton Stanley to Africa to hunt for David Livingstone. He also equipped the ship *Jeannette* for a disastrous polar expedition in 1879.

The senior Bennett presented news that was reliable but that leaned heavily toward the tawdry and sensational aspects of life. This brought Bennett's paper and his personal traits under fire. A widespread "anti-Bennett" campaign developed under the leadership of Horace Greeley, one of the best-known figures in American journalism. During the "anti-Bennett" campaign, Greeley made effective use of his New York *Tribune,* which had a higher intellectual and moral tone than the *Herald.* (It is interesting to note, in view of the Bennett-Greeley feud, that the two papers merged in 1924 to become the New York *Herald Tribune,* today an important newspaper giant.)

Greeley had begun his newspaper career at the age of

fifteen. Although his first New York venture, the *Morning Post,* was short-lived, his second effort, *The New Yorker,* started in 1834, soon became a popular and profitable weekly literary paper. In 1840, Greeley combined *The New Yorker* with another of his publications, the *Log Cabin,* to form the *Weekly Tribune.* Through it, Greeley soon became as famous as the people he wrote about.

Enthusiastic and outspoken, Greeley developed a modern editorial page which exerted wide national influence. His paper opposed the spread of slavery into the new western territories, and its vigorous anti-slavery policy was extremely influential in New England. Greeley, through the *Tribune,* also called for protective tariffs and legislation to outlaw the sale of liquor. He was a principal founder of the modern Republican Party and used his considerable power to get Abraham Lincoln nominated for the Presidency. After the Civil War he urged the North to grant pardons to all members of the Confederacy and vociferously attacked the weak administration of Ulysses S. Grant. Greeley had become such a famous personage that in 1872, nominated by Liberal Republicans and indorsed by the Democrats, he ran against Grant for the Presidency. Grant won a decisive victory and Greeley, broken in mind and body by the defeat, died shortly afterwards.

Greeley's protégé was Henry J. Raymond, who founded the New York *Times,* although it is only fair to say that it was Adolph S. Ochs who later elevated that newspaper to its present stature.

One of Greeley's most famous statements was, "Go West, young man, go West." Thousands of Americans took this advice, and in 1848, with the discovery of gold in California, the American population began a westward shift toward the Pacific coast. Railways were built, linking the East to the Middle West, telegraph lines transmitted messages across the Mississippi River, postal routes picked up speed. Aided by these growing forms of communication, hundreds of newspapers sprang up across the country, some born even before communities were settled. In the thirty years from 1830 to 1860, a total of about 1,800 new newspapers appeared in the United States.

Independent Period: 1872–1948. By the closing years of the nineteenth century, the American newspaper had become Big Business. Joseph Pulitzer, who had owned the St. Louis *Post-Dispatch* since 1879, was able to purchase the New York *World* for $346,000. Within five years, he had erected a $2,500,000 building and paid for it from his newspaper's earnings. Ten years after Pulitzer acquired the *World,* the paper's annual budget was over $2,000,-000; it had 1,300 employees. By 1897, its circulation had reached 1,000,000.

In the late 1880's, E. W. Scripps started a new concept in American journalism—the chain newspaper. In Cleveland, he started the *Penny Press,* which was the first of several papers he founded from the Middle West to the Pacific coast. Today his original chain has grown into a coast-to-coast empire, known as Scripps-Howard Newspapers, Inc.

Another well-known publisher at the turn of the century was William Randolph Hearst, who founded a chain of papers and magazines that is still a force in American journalism. As Pulitzer's chief rival, Hearst was most famous for taking advantage of the sensational tastes of newspaper readers, and making lurid reporting a characteristic of most of his papers. The feud between his *Journal* and Pulitzer's *World* was bitter, as each tried to outdo the other. Critics claimed that Hearst reporting was in bad taste, that it violated the privacy and privileges of individuals, that it defamed the reputations of honest men. News presented in such a sensational manner was dubbed "yellow journalism," a term derived from a popular comic strip of the day featuring "The Yellow Kid."

Whether or not Hearst's tactics were unscrupulous and lacking in taste, his sensationalism earned him a fortune. He continued to add to his string of newspapers and many years later entered the magazine field with *Harper's Bazaar, House Beautiful,* and *Good Housekeeping.* Like Greeley, Hearst participated actively in politics, serving as a member of the House of Representatives from 1903 to 1907.

After 1900, the American newspaper, as a commercial enterprise, reached its high point. By 1914 there were more than 15,000 daily and weekly newspapers across the country. Then came a marked decline.

During World War I, when the economy shifted to the national defense, a number of newspapers were forced to abandon publication. Beginning in the 1920's and continuing through the 1930's and 1940's, consolidations and mergers were plentiful as strong newspapers bought out their weaker competitors. The Second World War put an additional seventy-five papers out of business. Within the thirty-one years between 1914 and 1945 the number of newspaper companies had shrunk from 15,000 to 1,749.

Since 1945 the number of operating newspapers has remained relatively constant. Today there are only 1,760 daily papers in the United States, and even these are not free from pressures threatening their existence. Two financial headaches of newspapers are the increasing cost of production and a steady decline in advertising revenue.

Two-thirds of a newspaper's operating funds come from advertising. With the ability of television to reach millions of consumers in seconds, businessmen have put more and more advertising money into television and, consequently, less and less into newspapers. As a result, it has become harder and harder for a newspaper to make ends meet. It would surprise many Americans to know how close to the edge, financially, many of our major newspapers are in relation to their widespread influence and readership. Oddly enough, the financial status of most newspapers has little effect on their circulation. The Hearst Corporation, for example, reported that its New York *Mirror,* with the second largest circulation of any daily in the United States, lost more than $10,500,000 in the eight-year period before it ceased publication in October, 1963. Many other newspaper companies have failed financially at the same time that their circulation has reached record heights. Today, national circulation figures are at their all-time peak with more than sixty million readers a day.

II

TODAY'S NEWSPAPER

The 1,760 daily newspapers of America are an important cornerstone of democracy. As long as the United States plays a major role in shaping the destiny of the free world, the press will play a major role in shaping the destiny of the United States.

Newspapers—those huge collections of fact, opinion, and merchandise display, purchased each day of each week by nearly sixty million readers—can, at their worst, be self-serving and unreasonable, shallow and prejudiced. To paraphrase a favorite nursery rhyme, when an American daily newspaper is good it is very, very good, and when it is bad it is horrid. Unfortunately, many of the very good ones are "horrid" on certain occasions, although seldom do the bad ones turn out to be very, very good.

If there is a single truth about the newspapers of the United States, it is that they are committed to the proposition that dictatorship and a free press do not and cannot exist simultaneously.

Aside from this, the American newspaper is almost too complex and contradictory for definition. To many of its readers it is the only complete record of events in the community, the state, the nation, the world, and, of late, in outer space. It forecasts everything from the weather to the scores of football games. It is the judge of what should be worn to a social function and how much should be paid for a piece of property. In 1,461 cities of the United States, the daily newspaper is both the conscience of the community and its daily chronicle of events.

A good newspaper tries, by stating its editorial opinions, to educate the populace and improve the quality of government. For the good of its readers, it seeks to better the community's economic and social condition. (Ironically, the same paper may also publish such material as horserace entries and results, providing an impetus to illegal gambling that makes the poor man poorer and dishonest men richer.) There is something for everyone in the newspaper. One reader may hasten to scan the stock market tabulations to see how his investments are faring, another the horoscope to see what luck awaits him. Still another reader may turn first to the top news stories of the day, and then go to the editorial page for an interpretation of these events which may challenge or bolster his own opinion. How good is a dramatic presentation, a television show, or an art exhibit? Many people must read the opinion of their favorite newspaper critic before they are prepared to say. On the same page that displays the time schedule of television and radio programs may be a biting criticism that could destroy many of these programs forever.

A community is sometimes disturbed and offended because a daily newspaper seems to be unfairly criticizing a mayor or a police chief or a school superintendent by declaring that there are holes in the street, that crime seems uncurbed, or that classes are too large. But to this same community, the influence of the newspaper has helped bring better government or helped pass the school tax that permitted the hiring of more qualified teachers and the building of additional classrooms.

Prior to any discussion of what a newspaper is, emphasis should be placed on one thing it definitely is not. It is not infallible. Goethe might have had the reading public in mind when he wrote: "It is much easier to recognize error than to find truth. Error is superficial and may be corrected. Truth lies hidden in the depths." Most persons are willing to admit that six witnesses to the same incident will give a half-dozen accounts if each is asked for his own version. But these same people do not expect the professional newspaper personnel who collect, compose, and publish the news to be subject to error.

We hear much of a "free press" and "freedom of the press," but often we do not realize the significance of the phrase. Most large daily newspapers—the vast, overwhelming majority—believe it is their role in the community to give news without fear or favor, regardless of any special interest.

"What I would point out to you is that freedom of the press is your right as citizens and not mine as a publisher. Freedom of the press must depend on public opinion," said Arthur Hays Sulzberger, now Chairman of the Board of the New York *Times,* to a group of journalism students at Columbia University. "The newspapers of Nazi Germany continued to make money long after they had lost their freedom. But freedom of the individual died in Germany the day that freedom of the press perished. Wherever the press is controlled by government, the other fundamental freedoms go."

How frequently this has been demonstrated in recent years—from Havana to Moscow and from Cairo to Peking!

The guarantee of a free press contained in the Bill of Rights of the U.S. Constitution is more than a guarantee that people may read what they please. Freedom of the press also means the freedom of the editor to print what he desires, within the limits of truth and good taste. It is not, as so many readers seem to think, the right of any individual to get whatever he wants printed in the paper. Above all, a free press must be a responsible press, one that can protest with vigor and validity when either a government or a private group seeks to suppress or manipulate the flow of news for its own advantage.

"All our citizenry," said Mr. Sulzberger at Columbia, "would be prompt to defend any attack upon freedom of speech, freedom of religion, or freedom of assembly. The throne of liberty is four-legged, and freedom of the press is the fourth leg that completes the structure."

With this in mind, let us examine this enigma that is the American daily newspaper. Let us take a close look at this unique instrument that, in the same issue, brings to the homes of the land what is happening in the world of international politics and in the world of the comic strip characters.

III

HOW NEWS IS PRESENTED

Before television, and even before widespread radio news coverage, it was considered a matter of pride for a newspaperman to get a story faster than his rivals on other papers. Today, the electronic miracles of television and radio have made it impossible for newspapers to get headline news to their readers *first;* the public can simply snap a switch and see a news event while it is happening. Since they know they cannot get there first, newspapers have changed their tactics and now try to get to the public with the *most.* This means anticipation of an event and, once it has happened, interpretation of its meaning.

The primary reason for any newspaper's existence is to offer its readers the news. There is, however, a subtle distinction between three aspects of the news. What a reader can see or what he can easily verify is *fact.* What he learns about the news—the circumstances, the causes, and the human elements that give depth and meaning to the facts —is *background.* What he feels, or is made to feel, is *opinion.*

To report that the United States and the Soviet Union reached an agreement on a nuclear test ban is to state a fact. To explain why they were successful in reaching accord is to provide the background. To declare that it was a great step toward international peace is to offer an opinion. The guiding principle followed by every reliable, mature newspaper is that opinion is not part of the news.

It is to be reserved only for the editorial page or for a signed article. A newspaper has the responsibility to guide the consciences of its subscribers, but an even greater responsibility to avoid misleading the public by "slanting" what seems to be straight news.

One problem a newspaper faces in fulfilling its obligation of objective, disinterested reporting is the placement

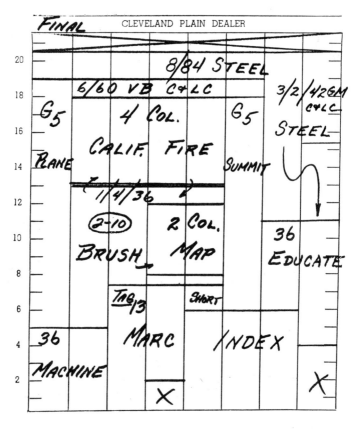

The layout of a newspaper front page, showing the amount of space to be devoted to each article.

of each article in the paper. Placement of a news item can sometimes achieve the same effect as distorted writing. By putting a less important event on the front page, the newspaper gives that event a significance it might not deserve. When this is done to advance the editorial opinions of the newspaper, it is considered highly unethical.

Another difficulty is that a newspaper averages over fifty pages in a weekday edition and each page has eight vertical columns. Few people stop to count, but there are roughly 150,000 words, not including advertising copy, in a single daily paper. Because the length of each article is different and advertising spaces vary in size, it takes the mathematical skill, ingenuity, and patience of the "layout men" to fit all the jigsaw parts of a paper together so that it is readable. The layout experts know that certain types of articles must go in specific sections of the paper. This enables the reader to turn quickly to his favorite section without having to search through the entire paper for something in which he may have particular interest.

A book reader usually starts at the beginning and reads each page until he reaches the end. The large American daily newspaper contains about the same number of words as a thick book, but its readers infrequently, if ever, read every word. In fact, even the most zealous readers rarely read every article—they have neither the time nor the desire to do so. Each member of a family might reach first for a different section or page. Sooner or later, each of them glances at the front page and each probably glances through the rest of the paper.

Depending on the day of the week, a newspaper is prepared in a varying number of sections. On Saturday afternoons and Monday mornings, there are usually only two sections, due to the comparative inactivity in local, state, and national business and government affairs over a weekend. On Sunday, however, the day when only one newspaper is published, there are often more than a dozen sections. People usually have the leisure on Sunday to read more, and the "Sunday paper," heavy and thick with news, features, comic strips, and supplementary magazines, has become a national institution.

The cream of the news appears on the front page: page one of section one. The most important story of the day is called the "lead story" and usually occupies the column or columns farthest to the right of page one. This story most often carries the biggest headline: a terse statement of the most important fact in the article. If the headline extends across all eight columns, it is called a "banner," a "line," or a "streamer." To provide variety and attractiveness, the front page (like most other pages) prints headlines in different type sizes and shades of darkness. As the importance of the article increases, so does the prominence of the headline type. This is also true of the article itself. If a story is particularly significant, its first few lines, or even its first few paragraphs, may be set in slightly larger type than the rest of the article. On occasion, an article is preceded by an emergency "bulletin," news that arrived after the paper had gone to press. A bulletin, colloquially known as a "bun," is a short statement of the most basic, and latest, information. A bulletin might be printed in dark (boldface) type and perhaps be set off by a box.

In many cases, the articles on the first page are so long that they are continued, or "run over" to inside pages. Very often, accompanying background stories appear on the same page on which the first-page article is continued.

The news editor, city editors, and other news executives consider carefully every story that has been written for an upcoming edition and make a thoughtful judgment about where each article should appear. They work closely with the layout department to see that news items are presented in proper perspective, so that the headlines are not "twice the size of the events," so that the public will not be misled, by the prominence of the display, about the relative importance or significance of a particular news item.

On an inside page of the average American daily paper are voiced the praise, criticism, or endorsements of the publishers and editors. This is called the editorial page.

A front page rolling off the press.

Since opinion has no place in reporting the news, the editorial pages of American dailies are carefully separated from the news articles. These pages contain from three to as many as seven editorials expressing the point of view of the publisher or editor. They also often carry letters to the editor from readers who care to comment on the news, on the paper's handling of the news, on the paper's opinions of the news, or on the thousand other subjects with which the letter-writer thinks the public

A Pulitzer Prize-winning cartoon, of the type that usually appears on the editorial page.

should be concerned. The editorial page usually features a regular political cartoon, satirizing prominent personalities or events of the day. Political analyses by nationally-known writers also appear on the editorial page, as well as the opinions of the paper's own columnists.

Throughout the paper is scattered local news and news of a general nature, from accidents to conventions, from weather reports to obituaries (articles about persons who have just died). Indeed, the "obits" are among the most widely-read of all the articles.

News items of special interest—sports, radio, television, movies, stamp collecting, bridge, gardening, books, musical performances, and art exhibitions—usually are carried in sections of their own or in a regular place in a section.

Weddings, engagements, and other local society news items are also set off by themselves in a section that includes stories about parties and about the activities of women's civic, religious, and social organizations. Additionally, there often appear, in this "women's section" advice-to-the-lovelorn columns, household hints, and recipes.

Toward the back of the paper is the classified section, containing thousands of small advertisements put in the paper for an established fee by individuals having no connection with the paper, except perhaps as readers. The classified pages include official notices of public hearings; houses for sale or rent; lost-and-found notices; lists of articles for sale or items wanted, from baby rabbits and rare books to furnished apartments and used cars. The classified pages are probably most often used by people looking for employment and by business firms or private persons who have positions to be filled. These are called the "help-wanted columns."

Money collected for classified advertisements constitutes an important part of a newspaper's revenue. Therefore, the business department is in charge of this section. Rates are fixed for the number of lines, or occasionally for the number of words, used. The longer period of time the ad appears, the lower the rate. An advertiser is encouraged to run an ad for several days to get the best response.

By far the most popular and widely read section of the American newspaper is that national institution—the comics. A comic strip is a series of pictures in a related order. A single picture is called a cartoon. Words spoken by the characters appear in enclosed spaces, called balloons, within the picture or, in the case of a single cartoon, a gagline explains the picture. The first well-known

A test-kitchen for trying out recipes, is part of the Women's Feature Department of a large daily paper.

newspaper comic strip was printed in the New York *World* in 1894. It was Richard Outcalt's "Origin of a New Species." Since then, the "funnies," as they are also called, have passed through several stages of growth. At first they depicted the pranks of little children and were intended only to be funny. Then they looked in on universal family situations, some of which were as sentimental as they were amusing. Later, they introduced the crime fighters and the "wonder men" who could perform superhuman feats. Today, they are leaning toward sophisticated satires of American life, or of humanity in general.

Newspapers generally obtain their comic strips and cartoons from a national syndicate (see Chapter IV), so that many comic characters have become celebrities by virtue of their exposure in papers all over the country. In fact, they often are more than celebrities; they are national heroes, who set patterns and customs for real people. When Joe Palooka, the good-natured prize fighter created by Ham Fisher, became the first comic character during World War II to put on a soldier's uniform, President Franklin D. Roosevelt personally thanked Fisher for helping to make the draft more palatable. Dick Tracy, the leading detective figure on American funny pages, has been a symbol of law and order since 1931. Al Capp's "Li'l Abner" strip is responsible for creating a holiday of sorts in "Sadie Hawkins Day," when American girls are supposedly allowed to pursue boys.

So many people in America read the comics that, during World War II, the strips were used to teach men and women in the armed forces. Favorite comic strip characters pointed out to soldiers who were learning other languages some of the difficult situations they could get into if they did not know the correct word.

Thus the newspaper, from banner headline to comics, offers its readers an enormously wide scope of material—to inform, to enlighten, to stimulate, and to entertain. Most of it is written by the newspaper's own staff of reporters, but no newspaper has a reporting corps large enough to give full coverage to the huge panorama of news. This fact will bring us to a look at the wire services.

IV

"LIGHT TO ALL CORNERS"

Mark Twain once said, "There are only two forces that can carry light to all corners of the globe: the sun in the Heavens and the Associated Press down here."

During Twain's lifetime, the famous abbreviation "AP" represented the only American news agency providing newspapers with up-to-the-minute coverage of world events. Today, the Associated Press and its younger brother, United Press International, "carry light to all corners of the globe"—to thousands of newspapers as well as to radio and television networks—minutes after an event has taken place, whether it is an international crisis in London, England, or a multiple birth in London, Ontario.

These two great wire services offer American and foreign newspapers an advantage they could not secure in any other way, by having correspondents and reporters in virtually every important city in the world. Using thousands of skilled newsmen whose millions of words travel through electronic circuits each day, in fifty different languages, AP and UPI make it possible for all of their customers to offer readers the most up-to-date news, no matter where it is happening. Some papers are prosperous enough to have their own bureaus in world capitals, but even these papers cannot station men and women everywhere at once. So they, together with less affluent papers, subscribe to either or both of the wire services.

The Associated Press was founded in 1848, when six

papers in New York City decided to share the cost of gathering news outside of the metropolitan area. It is still a nonprofit co-operative whose entire revenue is spent for gathering and disseminating the news.

The United Press was founded by E. W. Scripps in 1907, when he combined three regional newsgathering agencies in the United States. Scripps made United Press news available to all newspapers, as well as his own, thus making a handsome profit. By contrast, the AP was and is, as we have seen, a nonprofit organization whose members freely exchange news and govern the admission of new members' papers.

International News Service was formed in 1906 by William Randolph Hearst. It was originally created to provide news reports to morning newspapers, but when it later merged with other Hearst services, it began to operate around-the-clock, maintaining nearly a hundred bureaus in the United States and overseas.

In 1958 the directors of United Press and International News Service consolidated their resources and put both systems into one transmission network—United Press International.

Although there are historical and economic dissimilarities between the two major wire services, their newsgathering and distribution practices are fundamentally the same. AP and UPI newsmen and newswomen are "on the spot" whenever and wherever an event becomes news. Literally within minutes after a treaty is signed, a prominent person dies, a village is flooded, or an airplane is lost, AP and UPI flash their stories across the wires. They use their own telegraph, wireless, and commercial cables. In addition, they use more than five hundred thousand miles of leased land-line and underwater cable circuits.

Radio signals are picked up simultaneously in cities as far apart as Athens and Singapore, Johannesburg and Hong Kong, Moscow and Buenos Aires. The news is then transmitted in relay fashion; for example, the AP staff in London edits the copy it receives from New York and sends it on to AP offices on the Continent, where staff members translate the news into the local language and send it over circuits to subscribers in their country.

Newsrooms in newspaper offices and in radio or television stations have teletype machines which receive and print pages of completed and edited copy. Since the scope of the material is broad and the wire services produce a voluminous amount of copy, the local editors have to select the stories which will be most interesting to their own readers or audience. AP and UPI have extended their

Associated Press teletype machines bring world news to the smallest of American newspapers.

coverage to include feature material as well as current happenings, which requires additional selectivity among local editors.

The two services also transmit news pictures over their high-fidelity wirephoto systems. They also supply photographs through a technical process called "facsimile," by which a picture is reproduced through a radio broadcast. The transmitted signals are formed by a photoelectric cell that picks up the differences in light and dark in the subject matter as it is scanned by a beam of light. The signals are then converted into a facsimile of the original photograph by a mechanism attached to a radio receiver and are thus ready for the engraver.

Radio and television networks and stations, as we have seen, subscribe to the wire services as well as newspapers, and all use the facilities on a rental basis. These media do not pay for the amount of news they receive or use, but merely for the service of actually getting it. Monthly payments are made for rental of the electronic equipment and vary according to the number of circuits that are used. This money is used to maintain the operations.

There are other news services throughout the world, the most famous of which is the European service, Reuters, but none of them has either the facilities or the manpower to compete with AP and UPI. This fact does not render them useless in America, for their dispatches are highly respected and often cover areas that the American wire services do not.

As the newspapers become more sophisticated, their readers grow more demanding. If a paper has decided to offer political analysis, the public prefers to know the views of such experienced commentators as Walter Lippmann, James Reston, or David Lawrence, rather than the paper's staff writers. If the newspaper has decided to offer glimpses into the private lives of Hollywood stars, the public demands the "inside story" from such columnists as Hedda Hopper and Louella Parsons. Editors know they could never lure such people to their own staffs, but by subscribing to a news syndicate, they can print the columns of famous writers and thus attract more readers.

The syndicates are commercial operations which provide feature articles and columns for almost all American newspapers. These syndicates are different in many ways from the wire services: they do not deal in "spot" (or spontaneous) news, but offer papers material that provides background for the news or is written by columnists in special fields. A syndicate may handle a comic strip, a condensed book of general or topical interest, or a political column that analyzes the news.

Whereas wire stories are typed out electrically on teletype recorders, feature service material usually comes into a newspaper office by mail. It is called "time copy" because it is prepared well in advance of its publication date.

The amount of money a newspaper pays for a syndicated feature is based on the size of its circulation. A paper with a circulation of 200,000, for example, might pay $50 a week for a feature that would cost a small paper only $5 a week. Many syndicates are owned or controlled by large newspapers which originated features that became so popular that they are now sold to papers all over the country, and often outside the United States.

One of the earliest examples of newspaper syndication occurred in 1841. Moses Y. Beach, publisher of the New York *Sun,* helped pay the cost of sending a messenger for a copy of a Presidential speech by selling extra copies of the speech to his competitors.

Metropolitan newspapers cannot expect to have reporters at every place and at every time. Nor can they hope to have the most profound, best-known, or most humorous writers on their own editorial staffs. But, as we have seen, this is no excuse for a paper not to have first-rate news, features, and columns. If a newspaper cannot "carry light to all corners of the globe" by itself, it can at least reflect that light into every corner of its own community.

V

THE EDITORIAL STAFF

No matter what the size of a newspaper or the community it serves, the same precision is required of its staff. The newspaper must do its work not in weeks or days or even hours—but in minutes. It has to get the paper on the newsstands and into the homes of its readers in the shortest possible time after an event occurs.

Most newspaper staffs, regardless of their size, are divided into three principal divisions—"editorial," "mechanical," and "business." The editorial or news department gathers the news, writes it, edits it, and comments on it. The mechanical department puts the thousands of words of news stories and advertisement and the scores of photographs into print, folds the newspapers, and bundles them together for distribution. The business department is in charge of the newspaper's financial operation, from selling the papers and selling advertising space to paying salaries and negotiating with the ten or eleven labor unions to which employees of the newspaper belong.

The head of the editorial department is the editor-in-chief. Through his assistants—the most important of whom are the managing editor, city editor, and feature department editor—he oversees the main functions of his department. He and his staff gather, write, edit, and place the news in various positions on the pages of the paper and write the paper's editorial opinions.

The editor has the final word on what goes into his paper and, perhaps more important, what stays out. In addition to being a seasoned newspaper man, he should be a subtle diplomat in his own metropolitan world. Since his paper is the community conscience, he must be influential and reasonable enough in his editorial criticisms to arouse public concern. But his voice ought to be one of admonition, not of venom, for his newspaper reflects his character, strength, and personality. It is the editor's responsibility to protect the reading public from gross misinterpretation, inaccuracy, and distortion in the news that appears in his paper and the opinions his editorials express. The burden the editor carries is cumbersome but exhilarating. He shares it with his assistant editors, each of whom must be as responsible, imaginative, and resourceful as he.

The managing editor, second in the chain of editorial department command, is an executor rather than a formu-

Editorial policy decisions are made and discussed at editorial meetings such as the one pictured above.

lator of policy. His is one of the most important responsibilities in the editorial department: to see that the paper presents the complete picture, the broadest possible panorama of news at local, state, national, and international levels. He works directly with a group of sub-editors, each of whom is in charge of a separate department. Together they edit the news and decide how each story will be displayed on the page. This is called "playing" a story. A budget of a certain number of columns in each issue is allotted each editorial division, depending on the relative importance of the news that particular day. Thus, on one day, faced with a nationally important story, such as a Presidential declaration, the wire service (or telegraph) editor may be allowed twenty-two columns for his run of stories and the city editor only ten columns. The next day, the city editor, covering a hospital fire in his community may be allotted twenty-two columns and the wire service editor only ten. There are only so many columns for news, and they are allocated by the editor-in-chief according to his best judgment about the relative importance of each news item.

In order to determine the extent of this coverage, editors must be fully aware of all aspects of the local, state, national, and international situations. In order to keep abreast of developments in the nation's capital, most large newspapers maintain a Washington bureau. The chief of the Washington bureau heads an office which generally has men covering the Congress, the White House, the State Department, the Pentagon, and the various government departments. By telegraph and telephone, he and his staff file their daily stories, which are usually the most prominently featured news stories on the front page. But, as we have seen, almost all of the international news, and, in fact, much of the national news, is gathered not by the staff of the paper but rather by one or both of two major private news services, the Associated Press and United Press International. From all points of the globe, a million words pour daily into thousands of news offices through electronic teletype machines. The news that comes across the wires is much too voluminous to include in its entirety. As a matter of fact, most of it is important only to a specific metropolitan area or region. The telegraph editor must decide which of the "wire" stories the paper will use and at what length.

The city editor is responsible for the gathering, writing, and editing of all local news. He is the director of the large staff of reporters, rewrite men, and photographers who ferret out the news and take pictures. He makes the assignments and discusses them with the reporters. To be sure, he must have a "nose for news," but he must also possess qualities of leadership, judgment, and charm. He is the mentor, the critic, and the father-confessor of every reporter who covers the local community. Consequently, a beginning reporter learns more about the facts of newspaper life from the city editor than from any other man he will meet in the business.

The state editor is in charge of news originating within a state but outside the paper's city. Larger papers not only have correspondents in each of the major cities of their state, but also regular or contributing writers in small towns. Coverage of the activities of the state legislature and the state capital is one of the most important aspects of the state editor's job. But general news of interest to a particular town is important, too. News of this sort often is placed on one or two pages of the paper and carried only in the edition which is sent to that community.

Also directly responsible to the managing editor are the editors of special departments. They handle such subjects as sports, business, society, television, radio, drama, movies, real estate, religion, and shipping news. All of these editors are specialists in their fields. Except for the sports editor, they do not have "editor" status in the executive sense. But neither are they general reporters, since they are seldom called upon to do anything outside their special department.

Finally, there is the Sunday and feature editor, third in importance to the editor and managing editor. He reigns over a domain that is separate from the regular news organization. He is the head of a large staff—almost a newspaper within a newspaper—which puts together the large Sunday paper. The material he has to organize is voluminous, perhaps five times as large as the daily paper. It is also of a considerably different nature. It is mainly feature material—longer articles, essays, humorous stories—as opposed to the daily newspaper's "hard news" items. The Sunday editor often has the responsibility of buying for the paper nationally syndicated comic strips and columns. Although his paper is unusually thick, the Sunday editor enjoys one advantage. He has more time to prepare his copy—or "meet his deadline." Almost all material in Sunday papers, exclusive of the first section of news, can be prepared and printed days in advance.

This, then, is the basic structure of the editorial department, the heart of any paper, no matter how slight its influence or how small its circulation.

VI

THE CITY ROOM

To a person unfamiliar with its workings, the "city room" of the typical American daily newspaper is a disorganized, confusing place. It is the general headquarters of the local newsgathering forces. Here one finds long rows of desks, each not much bigger than the typewriter it contains, at which the reporters sit, wading through notes as they compose their articles. There are also much bigger desks, fortified with telephone switch boxes, spindles of news copy, wire baskets, and stacks of newspapers —bastions behind which sit the supervising editors. And here, finally, is a massive table, sometimes kidney-shaped, sometimes formed like a "T," adorned with paste pots and big scissors, galley proofs and clipped newspapers, around which work members of the copy desk, the anonymous but invaluable men who read and put headlines on the reporters' articles.

Through the noisy hum of the room is the staccato of many typewriters. A shrill voice screams "Boy!" to attract the attention of an office boy. A city editor summons a reporter forward by shouting a surname. Reporters dash to or from assignments with an accompanying photographer hard on their heels. No one ever talks softly and hardly anyone ever walks, which is what often gives a false impression of confusion and inefficiency. Actually, the organization of a news room, or city room, is so fundamentally simple that it would delight an efficiency expert.

The control center is the city desk. Here a reporter receives his assignments and turns in his story, or "copy." From the city desk the article proceeds to the copy desk, where any grammatical errors are corrected and headlines are written. On a metropolitan newspaper, the various size and type headlines go by number. These are kept, so to speak, in stock. A No. 22 headline, for example, may be that which the newspaper uses for a two paragraph "short" story. A No. 13 headline could be the bold type that would be placed on a disaster story. Since the story

A typical front page of a daily, tabloid-type newspaper. The page is smaller than in most papers, and the headline type is larger.

itself (always typewritten) and the headline (usually written in soft pencil) are sent by the copy desk to different parts of the composing room, they must each bear an identifying mark that will serve to unite them when they are ready to be set in type and placed in a page form. This identifying mark is called a "slug." The "slug" is literally the metal bar of type pulled out when the headline and story are joined together in print. No matter how important or how insignificant the story is, a reporter plainly marks his copy with a slug. If it is a weather story, in the upper left-hand corner of the first page of the reporter's copy, will appear the phrase "Lead Heat" or "Lead Flood" or "Lead Cold." Subsequent pages of copy will read: "First Ad Lead Heat" and "Second Ad Lead Heat." The word "lead" means what the story is about; "ad" stands for "addition." A cardinal rule of newspapering is that the copy desk, which tells the reporter how to slug his lead, must keep that slug short enough to fit easily on one line. That is why a weather story becomes "Lead Heat" or "Lead Cold." When a reporter has become firmly established as a star of the staff, his copy is slugged with his name or "by-line."

The city desk gives assignments each day to two kinds of reporters. Those who regularly cover a particular location or subject are known as "beat men." Those who cover varying types of stories are known as "general assignment" reporters.

The "beat men" cover such potential news sources (or "beats") as the City Hall, Courthouse, Federal Building, Board of Education, and various local government agencies. Often, they will go directly to their beat, checking in with the city desk by telephone, since much of the news that happens in their jurisdiction cannot be assigned in advance. These reporters are held responsible for any news development on their beat. On some big city newspapers, there may be several reporters assigned to the same beat—the City Hall for example—because there are so many departments and individuals to cover. When this is the case, there is a head reporter to co-ordinate the team's activities. The reporter who becomes thoroughly familiar with every aspect of his beat will be as well informed about the responsibilities of government as the officials who administer them. Such a newsman is an invaluable asset to his paper and community. By offering informed suggestions and criticisms to conscientious office-holders, he may be an influential, constructive agent in shaping the course of government, as well as in reporting it. Many times such a reporter has contributed to social progress. Relying on his experience to give him a broad perspective of the political or economic climate, he may give a hint to the mayor that the time is ripe for stepping in to mediate a labor dispute, to fight for lower electricity rates, or to start a public welfare campaign. Some of America's most progressive ideas were put into action by reporters or editors who literally put ideas into an official's head.

But there is an inherent danger in this procedure, and a reporter must be motivated only by his conscience. It is obvious that the worst kind of trouble could ensue if a trusting official depended on the counsel of a reporter who sought favor for his own gain or for the commercial gain of others. That is why many of the most experienced and wisest of American reporters are the most hesitant to offer suggestions to the news sources they cover.

"General assignment" reporters face no such quandary. Each day when they check in, they are told what specific event to cover. It may be a speech by an important visitor to a local club. It may be a feature story about an individual with an interesting and unusual hobby. Or it may be that the general assignment reporter will be rushed out to a major "spot news" development, such as an airplane crash, a murder, or a big fire.

The basic plan of operation employed in the city room, where reporters and the photographers clear their work through a central desk, is the same throughout every department of most U.S. metropolitan newspapers.

All parts of the news-gathering machinery have access to the newspaper's library, called the "morgue," where pictures and information about past happenings are kept. The library of a big paper contains so much detailed information about so many subjects that, it has been said, "it keeps compiling more and more about less and less until ultimately it knows everything about nothing." Obvi-

The City Room of a large metropolitan newspaper.

ously, however, without past records, obituaries, pictures, and other material in a library, a reporter could not function properly. A newspaper library formerly occupied a vast amount of space but now, because of a photographic process that enables a full page of a paper to be reduced to a half-inch square of film (to be magnified on a screen when needed) less room is required and more information can be stored away.

No matter how well organized a newspaper may be, nor how competent its staff, there is a lot of luck involved in news coverage. If a major event happens in the early evening it is advantageous to the morning paper. If it happens at noon, the afternoon papers get the first story. Neither the editor nor the reporters can control what happens, when. Much of the important news, however, is the result of the most careful planning and probing of sources. In this area, both the reporter and his city editor keep a comprehensive calendar far in advance of everything that is scheduled to happen. When the day comes, the reporter is fully prepared to cover the event.

Now let us take a closer look at that heterogeneous, hard working, often intriguing group of men and women who carry the pass of "the newspaper guy."

VII

THE REPORTER

One of the legends of the American newspaper is that it is only as strong as its staff of reporters. This is only partly true. Reporters certainly are the strength of the organization. They are the quick, and, it is to be hoped, accurate observers who present to readers substantiated facts instead of vague rumors or prejudiced opinions.

But there are other highly important parts of the newspaper structure, including the city desk personnel, who give the reporters their assignments for articles, the copy desk workers, who edit articles, and the unsung heroes of the composing room make-up crew. There also are the news photographers, who really are reporters in every sense except that they tell a story with a camera instead of words. No employee of a metropolitan newspaper works harder for less money and less sympathy or under more difficult conditions than a photographer. A reporter can make a typographical error and it will be corrected by the city desk. But if a photographer errs with his camera, the picture that could have told a story better than hundreds of words is lost forever. If he succeeds in getting the picture, under the most harassing circumstances of crowds and weather conditions, one tiny mistake in the darkroom where he is developing his print can destroy all his efforts.

Still, the glamor people of the newspaper world unquestionably are the reporters. In Europe, the word "reporter" does not have a very lofty meaning; there, it is the "journalist" who counts. In the United States, a person who describes himself as a "journalist" is immediately suspect, regarded as a semi-professional at best, or a pompous fool at worst. (An old American definition of a journalist is a person who goes around borrowing money from reporters.)

Thanks to fiction and the movies, the reporter is a much more glamorous figure outside his own office and profession. Reporters on big American daily newspapers receive salaries ranging from $75 to $300 for a five-day, eight-hour-a-day work week—depending on experience, ability, and the wealth of their employer. This is frequently less money for harder work than that received by members of editorial and business staffs whose identities are usually unknown to the public.

City editors have long agreed on at least one of the most necessary attributes of a good reporter. They say he must have an excellent "pair of legs." In the parlance of the press, "a good pair of legs" means the disposition to leave a desk and a telephone and a comfortable office and move on to the actual scene of a story or talk face-to-face with persons involved in a story. In short, it means the desire to get up and go, to get out and move around. Certainly as necessary to a newsman is an insatiable curiosity. This requires more than an inquiring mind. It requires a burning compulsion to know, a willingness to ask hard questions in order to find out not only about the important matters but also about what seem to be trivial details.

A good reporter must have the intellectual integrity possessed by the serious practitioner of any profession. Some call this integrity objectivity—the ability to see both sides of a story and to refrain from becoming personally involved. It is that, but it is also an honesty of the mind. It is the kind of temperament which will not react to insult with anger or to anger with insults. The reporter must continually remind himself that he is a disinterested chronicler of the facts. As such, he should strive to give a full, accurate, and unbiased account of what has happened. A good reporter is as much interested in the missing segments of a story as he is in what he already knows to be fact. To get the complete account, then, he must ask questions, sometimes deftly and tactfully, always probingly. Since the daily newspaper is a history of the world's happenings on a given day, the reporter must know as much as possible about the world in which he lives. He needs as much education or background information as he can get. Above all, he must cultivate many friends or acquaintances, for his most important source of news is what he is told; thus his acquaintances are vital to his success.

Probably every young person who has any facility for writing, who is gifted with imagination, and filled with the desire for adventure has, at one time or another, fancied himself a reporter. With the competition for reporting jobs as keen as it is, how can a youth convert this dream into reality?

The boy or girl who yearns for a career in journalism has probably begun as an editor on his high school or college newspaper. He should have been writing and reporting long before he has had any formal training. By the time he reaches college age, he should know whether he wants to make a career of newspaper work. If he does, he should plan his studies to give him the broadest possible educational background. Most city editors now prefer to hire applicants with a strong liberal arts education, with emphasis on English, history, and the social sciences. Others prefer to hire students directly from journalism school, which offers specialized training in techniques of reporting. While in college the aspiring reporter should try to get as much writing and editing experience as he can, either on the college newspaper or on one of its magazines. Some colleges and universities require work on college dailies or weeklies as part of journalism courses; in others, such work is optional. The most important thing for a prospective reporter to understand, however, is that the mere fact of having worked on a college newspaper does not qualify him for a position on a large metropolitan newspaper. Even a sense of what constitutes the news and a broad educational background are not guarantees for obtaining, or succeeding in, a newspaper job.

The greatest frustration of college graduates seeking reportorial employment is being told, "Come back to us after you've had practical experience." Where does this aspirant, having completed at least four years of college, get this "practical experience"? He may try a local weekly paper, one of many small neighborhood papers in America whose copy is largely social news and advertising, or he might try to get a public relations job with a business firm in which he is responsible for putting out a "house organ," a publication directed to the employees of the organization.

Many successful newspapermen and women have done none of these things. They got hired by simply refusing to accept "no" from the employing authority—but without being offensive or importunate. With persistence and firmness, they asked the city editor for a job again and again. They offered to take any job, just to give them a chance to prove their worth to the staff. This sort of perseverance, if handled with complete self-control, reflects determination, tenacity, and initiative—three more requisites for a reporter. Many times, a city editor, impressed by the young person's dedication, may finally give him an opportunity.

The "police beat" staff is the "nursery school" for most reporters. By covering the happenings at local police stations the young reporter learns how to get facts and what to do with them. He begins to learn what facts *are*—not opinions, and not half-truths. He begins to develop personality, responsibility, and technique. And, in the rudest lesson of all, he learns what a complex and frequently unpleasant business life itself is. Working at police headquarters, the "cub" reporter faces drudgery and routine in his efforts to dredge up small items of news. He sees the tragic and unpleasant side of life, for police stations are not places where happy people ordinarily go. He learns something about prostitutes and burglars, murderers and narcotics addicts. He learns how to wheedle information out of taciturn policemen and firemen, how to persuade grief-stricken relatives to lend pictures or reveal details about the lives of loved ones who have been killed or injured. Through these grim glimpses of life, the young "cub" reporter masters newsgathering technique and routine. He learns how to search through the reports at the central police station, how to check on each new assignment made by the detective bureau, how to watch and check each police call, and how to "call the rounds"—telephoning a selected list of hospitals, the county morgue, the city jail, the suburban police and fire stations.

After about eighteen months on the "police beat," he

acquires a sense of the news, and the skills needed to report it. He has learned the fundamentals of accuracy, especially that he must verify spelling of names and addresses. He discovers that the smallest error may result in libel action against his newspaper, so he refuses to take the word of others but determines to find the facts for himself. In any questionable case, he knows he must check the official records. Prying facts out of people who are frequently unwilling to give them is an exasperating business, but it schools the young reporter in patience and perseverance, in tenacity and diligence.

He learns that Rule Number One for a good reporter is always to suspect the worst. This may seem a cynical attitude, but police reporters deal so frequently with human frailty that they learn to expect it. He learns that most people like privacy and those who seem anxious to have a story printed often may have an ulterior motive. Conversely, he learns that when anyone tries to suppress a story without a legitimate reason, a conscientious reporter must redouble his efforts to find out why. Increasingly a judge of human nature, he learns when to suspect a person is not telling the truth. He becomes a diplomat with a sense of humor, a compassionate man who treats everyone, no matter who they are, as human beings. Yet he never becomes emotionally involved with them or forgets that they are primarily potential news sources.

By far the most important lesson the young reporter can learn in his early training are the ABC's of newspaper work, the "Who," "What," "Where," "How," and "Why" of a story. The beginning reporter, having become sensitive to the "Why," also learns that he is merely required to answer the questions raised by a story, not comment on them. His mission is one of impartiality.

By now, too, he begins to learn to develop news by making friends, by being a good listener, by memorizing details, by asking the right questions, by presenting unbiased answers, by weaving together seemingly isolated threads, by being persistent without being belligerent, by being tactful without being servile.

If he learns these rudiments, he is ready for what the newspaper considers its major reportorial assignments.

VIII

PUTTING THE PAPER TOGETHER

The most complicated process in publishing a large paper every day is putting the news into print. This procedure is handled by the mechanical department in four separate branches: the composing room, where the type is set; the stereotyping room, where casts of type-pages are made; the engraving room, where photographs and drawings are transposed into etchings and half-tones; and the press room, where the paper is printed, folded, and packaged for delivery. Let us take a look into each of these rooms and see what happens, step-by-step, in the printing process.

In the composing room, linotype operators set copy into type.

54

The Composing Room. When the copy written in the news room is ready for printing, it is taken to the composing room to be set in type, after which the type is arranged into pages. The sheets of copy are cut first into smaller pieces, which are called "takes," and then distrib-

Arranging type in a page form is done in the makeup department.

uted to the linotype operators to be set into type. A linotype machine casts an entire line of type in one bar and is operated from a keyboard which resembles a typewriter keyboard. These lines of type, called "slugs," are assembled in long metal trays, or "galleys," and are inked. Long sheets of paper are placed over the type and a roller runs over them so that their undersides take the imprint of the "galleys." These printed sheets are called "galley proofs." They are sent to proofreaders, who correct any typographical or spelling errors.

When the mistakes have been fixed, the trays of type go to a special branch of the composing room called the "make-up" department, which arranges the type as it will appear on the finished page and fits it into forms of newspaper page size.

Advertising copy is handled in the same manner except that some portions of it have to be set by hand.

Each full page of type is then placed within a metal frame called a "chase" and is locked securely in place by an arrangement of wedges known as "quoins." Heavy mechanical mallets pound a leather-covered block on the face of the type so that the type and the space for the photographs are perfectly even. The page form is then ready for the matrix from which stereotypes are made. The photographs will be ready for matrixing as soon as they leave the engraving room.

Engraving Room. Words have to be transposed into type, and type must be transferred to a special kind of mold. By the same token, photographs and drawings used to illustrate stories have to be translated onto metal before they can be printed. This is done in the engraving room.

Drawings, photographs, cartoons, and all other illustrations are classified together under the general heading, "art work." If the art work is a photograph, the picture is tacked to a board under the focus of a powerful camera which is large enough to accommodate a full-page plate. The photographer can reduce or enlarge the subject to the exact size needed for the finished newspaper. A screen is placed between the camera and the photograph so that the negative will represent shadings of light and dark. The negative is made in the usual manner and when it is dry, the image is transferred to a sheet of copper. This copper sheet is immersed in an acid bath, etched, and then mounted on a type-high metal base. It is matrixed with the type and made ready for stereotyping. If the art work is a pen-and-ink or crayon drawing, it is reproduced by what is called the "line process" and is etched on a zinc, instead of a copper, plate. Now both the type and the art work are ready for matrixing. The art work is sent back to the composing room.

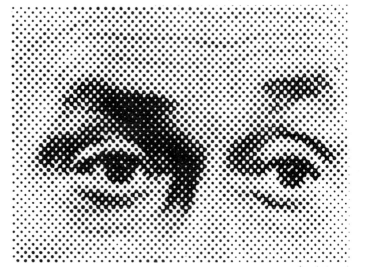

Detail of a newspaper photograph, showing the screen by which light and dark areas are indicated.

Newspapers of large circulation are printed on rotary presses that turn at high speed. Therefore, it is necessary to duplicate the flat page of type on a semi-cylindrical sheet of metal called a "stereotype," which can be attached to the press. The first step of stereotyping is the last step of composing, making a matrix, or "mat," which is a page-size sheet of thick papier-mâché that has been moistened and placed over the page form. Under hydraulic pressure, this sheet is pressed down while heat is applied so that when the moisture is driven off by evaporation, the sheet is baked dry. Consequently, a perfect impression of the page is made in a few minutes. The matrix is then taken to the stereotyping room.

The Stereotyping Room. When the matrix arrives in the stereotyping room, it is inspected and all defects are corrected. Then it is put into a semi-cylindrical form and rounded. The mat goes into a machine that contains molten metal. When the operator pulls a lever, the liquid metal pours against the matrix, and the machine releases a page of type in one solid piece of rounded metal called a stereotype, or "shell." As the stereotypes come out of the casting machine, a conveyor belt moves them on to another machine, which removes all irregularities and makes every edge and dimension accurate. The stereotyped page is now ready to be fastened to the presses.

The Press Room. When both the type and the illustrations have been processed in the composing, engraving, and stereotyping rooms, they are sent to the press rooms. Newspapers that have large circulations are printed on rotary web presses. Paper from large rolls flows continually through these machines, moving at high speeds, and coming into contact with the revolving cylinders, to which the heavily inked stereotypes are fastened. At a bell signal, the press cylinders start to turn, faster and faster, while the paper is fed through the roll from a revolving reel. When a roll of paper is almost used up, an automatic device cuts off the sheet and glues it to the end of a new roll. This change is made without stopping the presses.

The average size newspaper press can print, fold, count, and pack for distribution thousands of papers an hour, an impressive mechanical operation to watch. But compared to some of the modern machines available today, these big presses seem like antiques.

Early in the spring of 1963, the Oklahoma City *Times* announced that it had published its regular editions with type set entirely by a computer. This was the first of many American papers now using automatic typesetting. Thousands and thousands of words are pre-stored in a powerful computer in a special code arrangement on tapes. After

Rolls of newsprint ready to be fed into the presses.

a story is written, edited, and proofread the copy is punched into paper tape by a typist. The computer accepts copy in the form of electrical impulses. The tape is fed to the machine, which stores several lines of copy at a time in its magnetic core memory. The machine adds spaces to fill out lines evenly, hyphenates where necessary,

Newspapers coming off the presses have still to be cut and folded.

and produces a finished tape. The typist punches instructions to tell the computer when to indent for a new paragraph. When the tape is finished, it is then fed into an automatic linecasting machine which sets the type. The system can keep eight linotype machines busy simultaneously, setting eighty-five column-length lines per minute.

The Associated Press quoted the production manager of the *Times* and *Daily Oklahoman* as saying that the type-setting computers "could make the difference economically in the survival of many newspapers." Installing automatic equipment is economically beneficial to all large businesses. It can increase their efficiency and lower their costs. To newspaper owners these electronic machines appear to be a long-waited blessing.

As in other industries facing the question of automation, the mechanical employees of newspapers are members of powerful labor unions. Several big-city newspapers recently lost millions of dollars during a four-month-long strike that resulted primarily from the printers' refusal to work until management would award them better pay and, especially, a guarantee of job security against automation.

Electronic type-setting equipment has far-reaching implications for every newspaper in the country. If a newspaper can be produced in a shorter period of time, news deadlines can be pushed up and Americans will receive later news in their local papers.

IX

THE BUSINESS SIDE

Although they do their best to serve the community, American newspapers are strictly a private business, employing a total of nearly 350,000 people. There are no government-owned newspapers in the United States. As a commercial enterprise, the newspaper business ranks twelfth among America's principal industries. Funds running into millions of dollars are invested in a single newspaper operation. Presses, composing machines, and engraving equipment are enormously expensive. Some printing presses cost more than a million and a half dollars each. Many large metropolitan newspapers use as much as 125 tons of paper every day. One ton of this paper, called "newsprint," may cost $135. Producing a paper that sells less than 100,000 daily copies might demand only 700 workers; putting out a newspaper with a circulation of more than 500,000 copies a day may require the combined efforts of 3,500 people.

The business department is important to the strength of a newspaper, especially the advertising salesmen. Although very little credit or recognition ever is given these individuals, without their efforts there would be no income and, therefore, no money to publish and distribute the newspaper. Through their contacts in the business community, these men also play an important role in creating the "image" of the paper and, on many occasions, bring back to the office "tips" or hints that lead to the development of major news stories.

Advertising is the "oxygen" of a newspaper. Without it, the publication dies. The advertising manager has a bright and energetic group of salesmen whose job it is to keep advertising rolling in and to see that it is ready for the mechanical department for printing. Advertising space is offered to subscribers by contract and the longer the term of the contract, the lower the rates. A movie theater chain, for example, agrees to use 20,000 column lines of advertising a year. If, at the end of the year, this lineage has been exceeded, a reduced rate is granted by the business department. All advertising rates depend on the newspaper's circulation. The higher the daily sales, the higher the rates. This is logical, since advertisers should pay more to reach a larger consumer public. Usually, the advertiser submits his own copy and his own art work to the business department, which then sends it to the mechanical department to be matrixed, stereotyped, and printed.

There is no machine and no mechanical operation that can replace the human initiative, competitiveness, and precisioned timing of those people actually responsible for newspaper sales—the members of the circulation department. The word "circulation" refers to the number of regular newspaper purchasers—people who either receive their papers through home delivery or buy them at newsstands. The economics of a newspaper revolve around these sales. Consequently, the circulation manager holds a key position in the business department.

The circulation manager is in charge of distributing the paper, both within his own city and throughout the state. In large American cities where two or more papers compete at the same time of day, many thousands of sales might be made or lost during that precise minute it takes an edition to reach the customer. The circulation manager heads a corps of truck drivers and delivery boys who must meet their deadlines to keep the whole organization in business.

Newspapers also have an ambitious promotion staff

A member of the circulation staff measures a street on a map in order to provide efficient distribution.

whose job it is to keep the newspaper in the public attention. Very often, a circulation manager will authorize a special campaign in order to sell more newspapers. Some papers have contests, running for weeks at a time. These often take the form of puzzles, of which the reader has to correctly complete a certain number in order to win a prize. Thus he has to buy the paper every day. Publicity "gimmicks" other than contests can consist of the paper's sponsorship of popular local events, such as an annual Thanksgiving Day football game played for charity. The paper might not benefit financially from these promotions, but as a result of them it becomes regarded as a public benefactor and a dynamic instrument in the community.

The business department also administers the operation of the newspaper plant and supervises all purchasing. It handles personnel problems and is in charge of the payroll. Bookkeepers and accountants are as numerous as reporters. By distributing papers and soliciting new readers and advertisers, the business department keeps the publication firmly on its feet. If the business department fails to keep the paper solvent, then the editorial department can have no effectiveness. Although many newspapers can rightly be called a "public service," it cannot be denied that they are, first and foremost, a business venture.

X

TWO CHOICE ASSIGNMENTS

The newspaper business does not always seem as fascinating to those engaged in it as it is to outside viewers. Many veteran reporters will assure you that some of the most "interesting" people they have ever met have been neighbors, fellow customers at the supermarket, and others having no connection with reportorial assignment.

But within the newspaper world, or the "Fourth Estate," as it is called, there is no dispute that the most consistently fascinating assignments fall to those writers talented enough and lucky enough to be attached either to the Washington bureau of a large metropolitan newspaper, or to one of its offices abroad. In no other place on the newspaper (except perhaps in the sports department) is there permitted the freedom of writing style and, indeed, the freedom of personal expression encountered in Washington dispatches.

No group is prouder or more arbitrary and self-centered than the corps of 1,200 newsmen who cover Washington. This group can be divided into two segments. One is made up of the fifteen or twenty individuals regarded as White House "regulars" because they are permanently assigned to cover the President and news of his executive offices. The other is the several hundred correspondents who cover Congress on Capitol Hill.

Wherever the President of the United States goes, his

stopping place becomes the official White House. And wherever he goes, he is accompanied by the White House press, which has no official standing in law, but in practice receives more attention, greater privileges, and better accommodations than many governments tender their ministers and ambassadors. When the President travels by air, no plane is permitted to take off or land within ten minutes of his own plane which is designated "Air Force One"—no plane, that is, except "Air Force Two," which is the airliner chartered by the newspapermen covering the President. "Air Force Two" takes off immediately after the President's plane and lands immediately ahead of it. When the President travels by train, the White House press corps has its own special cars. When he goes by ship, the reporters are either aboard or in a following vessel.

While the expense of all this is paid by the individual newspapers, the same people who make arrangements for the President's trip handle arrangements for the accompanying press; a bill is subsequently sent to the individual newspapers.

Reporters covering both Presidential nominating conventions every four years follow rules set down by the Standing Committee of Correspondents, made up of five individuals elected by the Capitol Hill reporters. Assignment of coveted work space and seats at the convention is but a small part of the standing committee's responsibilities. It also supervises the day-by-day problems of press coverage of the United States Senate and House of Representatives. It should be noted that the rules governing the procedure of reporters in the political field are established by the reporters themselves, completely and entirely. As members of the White House Correspondents Association and the Senate and House Press Galleries, they choose from among themselves the officials who enforce the regulations the membership itself has approved. In no instance is there the slightest attempt at interference by the national government.

There probably is no institution in the world quite like a Presidential news conference. No other head of state, it can be safely said, allows himself to be asked questions about matters that often could be considered private—questions that sometimes are almost rude, and that are always submitted for the sole purpose of having the head of the United States government explain, clarify, defend, confirm, or deny.

The Presidential news conference is generally believed to have started in the administration of President Woodrow Wilson nearly a half-century ago. It did not fare too well at first. While the handful of reporters covering the White House was occasionally given an opportunity to submit their questions in writing and orally, the direct reply of the President was always "off-the-record." In other words, the Chief Executive could not be quoted in the newspapers without his express permission.

Presidents Coolidge and Hoover also gave Washington correspondents infrequent opportunities to submit questions (sometimes at private dinners), but it was not until the administration of Franklin D. Roosevelt, starting in 1933, that the Presidential news conference began to develop its present form. Mr. Roosevelt was exhilarated by the opportunity to match wits with White House reporters. He admitted them to his office one morning and one afternoon each week throughout his four terms. But still the "off-the-record" rule held. If Mr. Roosevelt happened to observe that it was a nice day, it was permissible to state:

"President Roosevelt yesterday commented that it was a nice day." But unless the President expressly authorized direct quotation, a reporter could not write:

"President Roosevelt yesterday said: 'It is a nice day.'" The reason for this restriction was that the words of the President of the United States were considered too significant and too apt to affect world affairs to take any chance of his being misquoted.

President Harry S. Truman continued the Roosevelt style of meetings with the press and even expanded them a bit. The Washington press corps became larger after the war, so there no longer was enough room in the President's own office for all the White House reporters to crowd in. Also, the Chief Executive no longer personally knew all his questioners. So the news conference was held most of the time in a large room in the Executive Office Building adjacent to the White House.

The news conferences became even more formal under President Dwight D. Eisenhower. They were held in the same big room but reporters now were required to wait until the President "recognized" them, usually with a nod of his head, before they could ask a question. Upon being given this nod, the speaker was obliged first to state his name and the newspaper he represented. (While this was intended to enable the President to learn the names of individual reporters and to give him an idea of how a certain answer might be received or treated by the paper, identification inspired a number of men to jump to their feet, not so much to elicit news by a question as to emphasize their own identity and their own knowledge.) But it was Mr. Eisenhower who first allowed sound motion pictures into the Presidential press conference.

A trademark of the Presidential press conference is the

remark, "Thank you, Mr. President," that always ends all questions and sends reporters dashing madly for the telephones. The senior representative of the Associated Press or United Press International, whichever has been assigned to the White House the longer, traditionally makes this statement and, when the President wishes to end the conference, he need only nod to this man.

When the late John F. Kennedy became President in 1961, he went a step further, moving the conferences into the huge State Department auditorium and allowing television cameras to record the conference as it happened. Since the outside world was "inside" the room as President Kennedy answered questions, it was no longer necessary to worry about direct quotation.

When Lyndon B. Johnson succeeded to the Presidency after the assassination of President Kennedy in Dallas, Texas, on November 22, 1963, it was immediately apparent that fundamental changes would be made in projecting the Chief Executive's image to the people of the United States and the world. Even though both men were dedicated to the same principles, even though both favored the same programs and policies, the personalities of John Kennedy and Lyndon Johnson were as different as their native Massachusetts and Texas backgrounds. Mr. Kennedy was the master of the quick rejoinder, the subtle touch. He seemed to do some of his best thinking on his feet, lightning-fast. Mr. Johnson's forte, developed during his many years of top legislative leadership, is friendly persuasion. He is at his best in give-and-take discussion, over the telephone or in small groups.

The question of whether President Johnson would continue the elaborate telecast and broadcast news conferences of his predecessor was soon answered. From the moment of Mr. Johnson's first conference, it was clear that he preferred the more informal methods of Franklin D. Roosevelt and Harry Truman. This conference was called without warning on a Saturday morning, when few regular reporters were at the White House, and it was confined to those newsmen actually present. They were ushered into the President's office for coffee, questions, and answers. The informality of the proceedings continued, but in different and more surprising ways. On one occasion, reporters covering a routine signing of a bill were suddenly invited to make a tour of the President's personal living quarters at the White House, with the Chief Executive himself serving as guide and dropping newsworthy items as he walked along. On another occasion, at his ranch in Texas, Mr. Johnson conducted a question and answer session during a barbecue for reporters. He stood in front of a microphone mounted on a bale of hay and the newspapermen, hands full of spareribs and cans of beer, interrogated him.

Probably the most romanticized of all newspapermen is the foreign correspondent. Literature, stage, screen, and television portray him as an irresistible combination of a master spy in a stylish trench coat, a cigarette-smoking investigator who knows more than an intelligence agent, as an incisive writer, and as an ardent lover who courts only heiresses and saloon dancers.

He may be a few of these things in small measure. He is more likely to be a first-class reporter who has been trained in his own country in the methods of his own newspaper, but one who has a deep knowledge of the history and the problems of the area he is reporting. Otherwise, he cannot recognize significant news when it occurs. A foreign correspondent also must understand fully how a news story breaking in a foreign area affects the interests of the United States and, particularly, the readership of his newspaper. This presupposes that the foreign correspondent is familiar with United States policies.

Since English is spoken in nearly all diplomatic circles and business communities throughout the world, it is not absolutely necessary that the overseas correspondent know a foreign language. Nevertheless, the reporter never will quite reach the people or understand their policies, aspirations, and problems unless he can speak with them in their native tongue. After English, the most useful language to know is French, highly valuable in Europe, Asia, and Africa. Then comes German, for Central Europe; and Spanish, for Latin America. Any other language is another tool and the more tools the correspondent has in his kit, the better workman he will be.

A word should be said about the so-called "instant foreign correspondent." This is the reporter who has grown up in the jet age and can get from one spot to practically any other spot in the world by jet airplane in two days. Such correspondents—and they are increasing in numbers rapidly—are merely as good as the background and experience they carry with them to their sudden foreign assignments.

XI

"THE FOURTH LEG"

We have seen that the American newspaper is a powerful influence in this country. What is it about the American newspaper which sets it apart from the foreign newspapers?

One of the more important differences is that American newspapers are servants of their local communities. The national newspaper is a rarity in American journalism. In the great majority of cases, the reader and the paper he reads are located in the same metropolitan area. That is a principal reason why the United States daily journal tends to emphasize local news over international stories. In a country such as Great Britain, which geographically is rather compact, it is not too difficult to publish a newspaper in London and circulate it to other large cities. But the vast distances in the United States, plus a time difference of several hours from the East to West Coasts, make it virtually impossible to publish a paper in Boston, for example, and distribute that paper in quantity the same day in San Francisco.

In some parts of the world, great daily newspapers are either completely government-controlled or are subject to government restrictions. In many countries, the press tends to be overwhelmingly sympathetic to the policies of the individuals and the party in political power. Even though American newspapers may support the candidate of a particular political party, they do not hesitate to criticize the policies and actions of that person or party when the occasion to do so arises. American newspapers can—and do—editorialize on behalf of a political candidate with the hope of getting him elected, but that man cannot control what is written about him or tell the paper what to write.

Joseph Pulitzer once claimed, "Our Republic and its press will rise or fall together." As our nation has developed from a group of democracy-seeking, fortune-hunting colonists to the world's seat of power and promise, so too, has the American newspaper grown from a few blanket-sized sheets of crude print to an unparalleled instrument of democracy and hope.

The American newspaper industry has had a dramatic history of its own, and produced many great men: Olympian figures such as Greeley, whose words shaped public opinion and government policy; cartoonists such as Thomas Nast, whose drawings were incisive enough to arouse public indignation and stimulate political change; correspondents such as Henry M. Stanley, Will Rogers, and Ernie Pyle, whose personal exploits and activities were news in themselves; and publishers such as Pulitzer and Hearst, whose bitter rivalry brought out talent and revolutionized news coverage.

Over the years American journalism has been elevated to a high professional level. Journalism schools recruit and train intelligent young reporters. Professional societies such as Sigma Delta Chi, the American Newspaper Publishers' Association, and the American Society of Newspaper Editors have raised the standards of reporting and newspaper administration. The American Newspaper Guild, a labor union for editorial employees, protects reporters and insures fair treatment for them. Pulitzer

Prizes, Nieman Fellowships, and other awards for reporting and writing keep competition among newspapermen lively and meaningful.

The American newspaper has made four major contributions to the profession of journalism. As the voice of a democracy and its chief protagonist, it has been a champion of freedom. As a newsgathering medium, it has used amazing skill and resourcefulness to bring up-to-the-minute coverage of world happenings to its people. As a business, it has become the twelfth major industry in the United States. As a profession, it has become one of the most envied, popular, and respected occupations in the world. These are not its only contributions, of course, but they embody the peculiar characteristics of the American newspaper. As was pointed out earlier, no accurate generalization can be made about the press of the United States except its unwavering dedication to the proposition that a free government and a free press are inseparable partners.

A modern newspaper building.

The American newspaper was born in order to gain freedom, was bred on freedom, and as long as it continues to exist it will be devoted only to freedom. The American newspaper is, indeed, the "fourth leg of the throne of liberty."

SUGGESTIONS FOR FURTHER READING

Ault, Philip H., *News Around the Clock*. Dodd, Mead, 1960.

Berry, Thomas E., *Journalism Today*. Chilton Books, 1958.

Bond, Frank Fraser, *An Introduction to Journalism*. Macmillan, 1954.

Higgins, Marguerite, *News Is a Singular Thing*. Doubleday, 1955.

Johnson, Gerald W., *Peril and Promise: Responsibilities of the Free Press,* Harper, 1958.

Lindstrom, Carl E., *The Fading American Newspaper*. Doubleday, 1960.

Mott, Frank Luther, *American Journalism,* Revised Edition. Macmillan.

Neal, Robert Miller, *News Gathering and News Writing,* Second Edition, Prentice-Hall, 1949.

Swanberg, William, *Citizen Hearst*. Charles Scribner's, 1961. (Paperback Edition, Bantam Books)

Sutton, Albert Alton, *Design and Makeup of the Newspaper*. Prentice-Hall, 1948.

Times, The New York, *News: The Story of How It Is Gathered and Printed*. The New York Times, Inc., 1949.

ABOUT THE AUTHOR

ALVIN SILVERMAN has been part of the American newspaper scene for more than thirty years. Since 1957 he has been Chief of the Washington Bureau of the Cleveland *Plain Dealer,* one of America's most influential daily papers. Before that, he successively served as education editor, City Hall reporter, State House correspondent and editorial columnist on the *Plain Dealer.* His coverage of American political life has taken him all over the world and earned him many honors for intelligent and responsible journalism. Mr. Silverman is a member of the Gridiron Club, an exclusive organization of America's fifty top newspapermen, as well as the National Press Club, the White House Correspondents Association, and Sigma Delta Chi, a professional fraternity of American newsmen.